101 FLY-FISHING TIPS

Lefty Kreh

THE LYONS PRESS

Guilford, Connecticut

An imprint of The Globe Pequot Press

10 9 8 7 6 5 4
Printed in Canada

Library of Congress Cataloguing-in-Publication Data
Kreh, Lefty
    101 fly fishing tips / Lefty Kreh.
    p. cm.
Rev. ed. of: Lefty's 101 fly fishing tips. 1999
ISBN 1-58574-035-7 (pbk.)
    1. Fly fishing. I. Title: One hundred one fly fishing tips. II. Kreh, Lefty.
Lefty's 101 fly fishing tips. III. Title

SH456 .K72 2000
799.1'24-dc21   99-058499

Photos by author.
Cover and text design by Donna J. Dove, K&D Limited, Inc.

Introduction

I have written this small book in hopes that it will make your flyfishing easier, increase your enjoyment of the sport, and you'll catch more fish. I have been lucky enough to fish around the world with many of the top fly rodders. From them I have obtained some great ideas. I also have lived by the philosophy that everything I do can be improved. I believe tradition is good for flyfishing, so long as it doesn't stand in the way of progress. Everything I do is subject to change and I am always looking for new ways to do things.

Many fly fishermen simply accept what is around them. If there is a worrisome problem, I always try to find a way to eliminate it. One example, cited in the book, are the straps that dangle from the hip boots that entangle the fly line. If you remove the strap from the buckle and reverse the buckle, then reinsert the strap, it is positioned inside the boot and the problem is eliminated. I hope you will find many such useful ideas in this book. And, if you come up with a neat idea, I'd love to hear about it

Have Fun with Your Fishing,

Lefty Kreh

Table of Contents

1 STORING YOUR LEADER END

A bothersome thing is trying to locate the end of the leader that has been wound on the spool. Most fly reel spools have holes or perforations in the outer edge. When finished fishing for the day, wind in all but about six inches of the tippet or

leader end. Insert this end through one of the holes, as shown in the photo. Simply push the end through and you can string up your rod on the next trip.

2 LOCATING THE TIPPET

It's frustrating trying to locate the end of a thin leader tippet, especially if it's a 5X to 8X and you are past the age of 40. There is a simple solution to this, however. The tippet is the thinnest

portion of your leader. Use a fairly large hook and locate the thin tippet. *Insert the hook under only ONE strand of the tippet.* It won't work if the hook captures two strands. Hold the hook securely and begin to wind as if you were recovering line. The spool will revolve and the hook capturing the tippet will chase around the thin monofilament until it arrives at the end. This is the same as if you held a rope in one hand and continued to pull the rope through your hand until you arrived at its end.

3 MAKE YOUR OWN REEL DRAG

If your reel is a rim control type you can make a superb drag with a small piece of leather. Cut a ping-pong paddle shape from an old leather belt, as shown perched at the top of the reel in the photo. Then, lash the paddle onto one of the crossbars so that the larger part of the paddle rests over the rim. When a fish makes a run, you can depress the paddle against the revolving rim and maintain an excellent, smooth drag. Using this paddle on a freshwater reel, I once landed an 86-pound tarpon.

4 IDENTIFYING FLY LINES ON REEL SPOOLS

The modern fly fisherman carries a number of reels with various lines on them. It's a good idea to label the spools. Line manufacturers now furnish an identifying label (shown on the left). But, if the line is placed on another spool, it's difficult to transfer the same label. Masking tape is durable and the numbers, when written with a soft carbon pencil or permanent pen, hold up well.

 5 ANOTHER METHOD OF MAKING A REEL DRAG AND BALANCING ONE

Photo 5A shows how you can modify reels that don't have a spool with a revolving rim. Use a metal cutting saw (sometimes called a saber saw) and carefully cut out a section as shown in the photo. Be sure that you don't damage or cut any of the parts on the inside. File the edges smooth and paint them. You can assemble the reel and push your thumb against the spool to get the desired drag.

Photo 5A

Photo 5B — An unbalanced fly reel spool (with one handle) wobbles badly on a high speed run by a fish. Balancing the spool is necessary. Buy a ¼ X 20 stainless steel nut from a marine store. Place a piece of masking tape on the underside of

Photo 5B

the spool, *directly opposite the handle*. Put a small amount of epoxy glue on the outside of the reel spool and gently lay the stainless nut in the puddle of glue. The tape prevents the glue from dripping through to the inside of the spool and can be easily removed after the glue has set.

 SETTING THE DRAG

Correctly adjusting the drag on your fly reel is vital to landing big fish. Most people depend on a mechanical drag, which they set too high. That's a bad idea. When the fish bolts away, if you point the rod at the fish and the drag is lightly set, you won't break the leader. I set my drag by drying my lips, and then gripping the line with my lips clenched as firmly as possible. I adjust the drag with clenched lips until I can no longer pull it from the reel. For additional drag, I use my fingers on the reel spool or trap the line against the rod.

7 LENGTH OF HAT BRIM IS IMPORTANT

Most anglers don't know that the length of a hat brim is very important in casting accurately. You may not realize it, but you monitor your cast while it is in flight. To prove this, make a few casts and notice how close you come to a target. Then, make several more casts and the moment the rod stops, close your eyes. You'll find that you won't be as accurate.

Repeat this experiment wearing a short brim and a long brim hat. You'll find that almost always the casts made wearing the longer brim are not as accurate. Also, when in a boat, a long brim hat tends to blow off your head much quicker than one with a short brim.

8 ANOTHER HAT TRICK

It is important to see many fish before you cast. Trout and bonefish are two species that quickly come to mind. Try another revealing experiment. On a sunny day, stand at an elevated place where there is clear water below. Without wearing a hat, peer into the water. You will see a limited amount below the surface. Next, put on a hat with a light-colored under brim. You will see more than you did with no hat. Now, exchange that hat for one that has a darker brim and you will see considerably better.

Sunlight, reflecting from the water's surface, bounces off a light colored brim and detracts from seeing what is below the surface. A dark under brim reduces the surface glare and increases your ability to see. You can effectively darken any hat under brim with black shoe polish, which will last a long time. Just give it a day for the fumes to air out before using the hat.

9 GREAT SHOE TRICK

This one tip is worth the price of this book! You will never have to tie shoes again. Shoestrings have trapped fly lines and ruined casts for thousands of fly fishermen. No longer is this a worry.

Remove the shoestrings from the shoes. Buy some 3/8-inch wide elastic at a drug store or sewing outlet. Cut an appropriate length and beginning at the top of the shoe lace the elastic toward the toe. Adjust the elastic to the proper tension so the shoes are comfortable but secure. Make a square knot to hold the elastic in place and clip the ends. Add a drop of glue to the knot to secure it. You will never have to tie these shoes again!

10 A HIP BOOT TRICK

Hip boot straps tangle your fly line and ruin your casts, as shown in the photo on the left.

The bottom photo shows that by removing the strap from the buckle, reversing the buckle, and reinserting the strap, the strap now lies inside the boot out of harm's way.

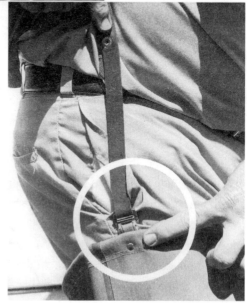

SHOULDER STRAPS FOR HIP BOOTS

Suspending your hip boots on your belt is not a good idea. Buy a shoulder harness designed for hip boots; they will stay up better and are much more comfortable.

12 DRYING HIP BOOTS WITH COFFEE CANS

Turning hip boots upside down to dry them is not the best idea. If they are positioned upright, the air circulates better, drying the boot faster. To do this you need to hold the boot open. Remove the top and bottom from a one-pound coffee can and insert it into the boot to hold open the boot. When traveling, flatten the can (see bottom right of photo); when ready to use, squeeze the can back into its normal shape.

13 DRYING BOOTS WITH A HAIR DRIER

A hair drier is one of the fastest ways to dry boots. *It's important that you do not use heat — just blow dry with cool air.* Heat will often ruin the rubber in the boots.

14 LOCATING LEAKS IN BOOTS AND CHEST HIGH WADERS

Finding a leak in boots or waders can be difficult. Take the boot or wader into a dark room and place a flashlight inside the boot or wader and move it around. The leak will soon show. Mark it immediately, so you can find it in a bright room.

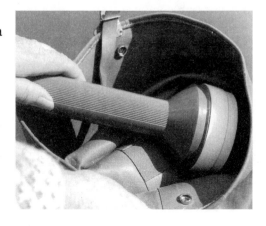

A FURNACE IS BAD FOR BOOTS

Never store boots near a furnace as shown in this photo. A furnace gives off ozone, which is bad for rubber materials.

CLEANING YOUR EYE GLASSES

There are many eyeglass cleaners. None are as good, I think, as alcohol swabs, available in most drug stores. These are little, soft patches of alcohol-saturated cloth stored in a water-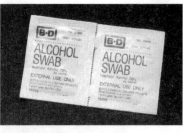

proof package that is a little larger than a postage stamp. The alcohol will remove salt crystals from your glasses, as well as sunscreen and a host of other dirt. Approximate cost is less than two cents for a swab. You will find many other uses for them.

17 USE DIFFERENT POLARIZING GLASSES

Pictured here are different kinds of polarized glasses. The one on the left has a pair of magnifiers in the bottom for people who see well in the distance, but have trouble close up. This same pair of glasses has a blue/gray color tint. Many people prefer this color for offshore fishing. The middle pair has a yellow/brown tint, which most experienced fly fishermen believe is the best all around color for fishing. The glasses on the right have a bright yellow color. I find these superior for fishing on heavily shaded trout streams and on rainy or overcast days. They are also superb glasses for night driving.

18 TILTING THE HEAD HELPS

Polarized glasses are manufactured to remove surface glare from water *under average conditions*. Many times you can remove additional glare by tilting your head as Sarah Gardner is doing here in the photo below.

19 VELCRO ON YOUR SUNGLASSES HELPS

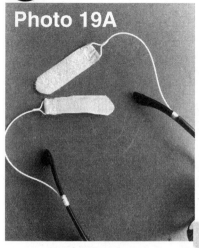

Photo 19A

Sunglasses have a bothersome way of constantly sliding down on the nose, especially in hot weather.

Photo 19A shows how to attach Velcro to the frames with a short length of fly line or other string.

Photo 19B shows the strings and Velcro attached and ready to be used.

Photo 19C demonstrates how you can adjust the two Velcro tabs to the correct position by pushing them together. The advantage of

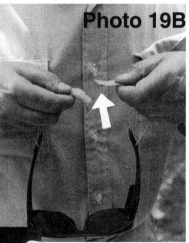

Photo 19B

this method is that the glasses can be adjusted for a loose or tight fit. Once the Velcro is secured, the glasses will never move.

Photo 19C

20 MEASURE WITH A BILL

There are many times when you would like to measure something. If you have a 1, 5, 10, 20 or a 100-dollar bill, you can use it as a measuring tool. A dollar bill is a fraction more than six inches long. Folded in half it is about 3 inches long, and folded again about 1 ½ inches long.

21 PHOTOCOPY YOUR PASSPORT

If you travel out of the country, be aware that there are people who may steal your passport. Photocopy the page in the book with all pertinent details on it, then, if your passport is stolen, you can use the copy to supply information to a local U.S. Consul.

I had my wallet stolen here at home and it took three weeks to replace all the papers, cards and other information in my wallet. Now, I photocopy my credit cards, health insurance, auto insurance and many other cards I carry. It sure makes it easier when you have to replace them.

22 WEAR SUNGLOVES

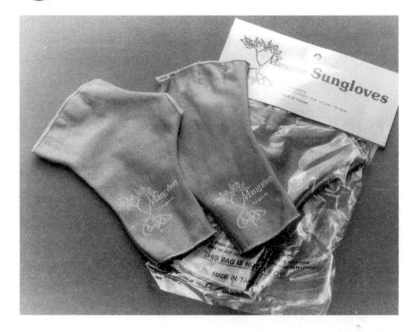

When I got a job in Miami in 1964, Joe Brooks, a famed outdoor writer, warned me to be aware of the dangers from the sun. "Wear long sleeve shirts, long pants and a hat," he cautioned. What he didn't tell me was to protect my hands. I have paid for that by having a series of skin cancers burned *only* from my hands. The photo shows sungloves that are inexpensive and I recommend wearing them when outdoors.

23 CARRY BAND-AIDS

Carry two or three Band-Aids in your wallet. I can't tell
you how many
times I have
used them.
Good not only
for small cuts,
but they also
protect your
finger when a
line is being
stripped across
it. I even
secured, for

the day, the foot of a rod guide with a Band-Aid.

24 DON'T DISCARD MONOFILAMENT

Never throw any monofilament on the ground. Take it
home with you or burn it. Even a six-inch strand of tippet
material can cause death. Birds use it for nesting material and get
entangled and die.

PLASTIC PIPE MAKES AN INDESTRUCTIBLE TRANSPORT CASE

Goop, other glues, sunscreen and other fragile containers taken on a trip, can be protected in a section of plastic pipe. I once had an airport employee run over my baggage, which squashed a tube of Goop — gluing most of my clothes together. After that I used the plastic pipe for storage.

26 A GREAT WINTER GLOVE

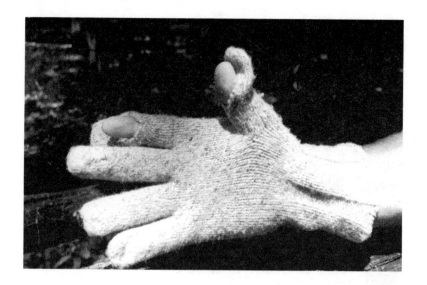

I have tried many types of gloves when fishing in cold weather. None of them kept my fingers warm. Many years ago I did something different. Using a pair of really fine wool gloves, I sewed a buttonhole in the tips of the fingers used for casting and fishing. You can install a Velcro tab on the back of each fingertip, so it can be folded back and secured in place. Even when wet, this type of glove keeps the fingers warm.

27 PLASTIC BAGS PROTECT YOUR CLOTHING

Anytime you are on a trip where your clothing may get
wet, store them
in plastic bags.
The bags
containing your
daily paper are
ideal. On several
trips I have been
the only one that
had dry clothing
in camp.

28 A SAFETY GRIP FOR YOUR PLIERS

Connect a short length of stout line between your plier
handles. It serves two
purposes. First, to get
the pliers out of the
holster quickly,
simply slip your
finger under the loop
and pull. Second, to
prevent the pliers
from falling out of
your hands and
overboard, keep a
finger tucked around
the line when using
the pliers.

29 FLY ROD TUBE TIP

Two simple chores will make it easier to use your rod tubes. The bottom tube in the photo shows that you can put a handle on the tube by using two adjustable hose clamps and a piece of strapping or rope. This serves two functions. First, it helps you to carry the tube. Second, when placed on a flat surface, it prevents the tube from rolling around.

Fly rod tube caps are easily lost. To prevent this, drill a hole in the center of the cap, then insert a length of heavy monofilament in the hole. Make a knot on the monofilament resting on the inside of the tube to keep it from pulling out. Make another knot on the other end of the mono and secure the mono with a cable tie. A drop of epoxy or hot glue will hold the cable tie in place. Total length of time to do such a job is maybe ten minutes — time well spent.

30 LABEL YOUR ROD BAGS

If you have several fly rods, individual bags are made for each rod. By labeling your rod bags you know which bag to put them into — and in a camp, you also know which bags are yours.

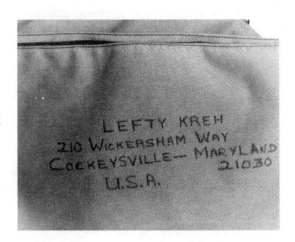

31 USE A METAL SCRIBE TO MARK TACKLE

Some people may object to this, but for years I have been using a metal scribe to put my name on my fly rod reel seats, fly reels and other items. There is never any doubt which tackle belongs to you.

32 ROD HANDLES

The *cigar shaped handle* is used on most small rods, especially for trout fishing. This is mainly because manufacturers think such handles are cosmetically more pleasing on small rods. These handles tend to move away from the thumb on the forward cast. That's okay for short distance casting, but the cigar handle is not recommended when using large rods.

When casting larger lines, flies or a long distance, the *half-wells style handle*, shown below, is recommended over the cigar shape.

33 LUBE YOUR ROD WITH A CANDLE

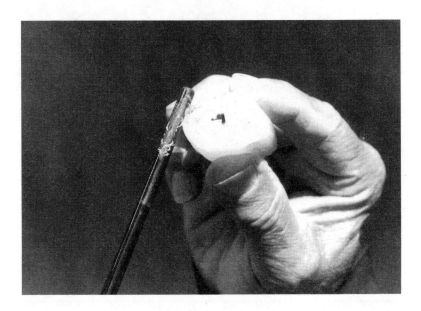

The male portion of any fiberglass or graphite rod needs to be lubricated occasionally, so the female section will be held firmly. Many lubricants have been used, but experience has taught me that a candle works best. The combination of the wax and oil tends to stay on the rod for a long time. Anytime you feel the male section is very dry, apply the candle — usually once a year is enough.

UP AND DOWN LOCKING REEL SEATS

There are two choices in fly rod reel seats: uplocking and downlocking. The downlocking, shown at the top of the photo is the least desirable. The butt of the rod rests at the base of the reel. The uplocking reel, shown at the bottom of the photo, positions the reel away from the end of the rod to form a butt extension. In this case, an additional short extension has been added. This allows the angler to position the butt of the rod against the belly when fighting a fish and allows the reel to be used more easily.

35 PROTECT THE ROD WHEN INSERTING IN THE TUBE

Allowing a fly rod to plunge down into a rod tube can create a problem. If a guide strikes against the side of the tube, it may pull a foot loose. Instead, place your fingers around the rod and slowly lower it into the tube.

36 TAKING APART A STUCK ROD

To take apart a stuck rod *you need to pull on both sections, evenly and in a straight line.*

If you have no help, the best method of applying tension in a straight line is to place the rod behind your knees. Grasp the rod with a hand on each side of the ferrule. Slowly spread the knees apart.

37 TAKING APART A STUCK ROD

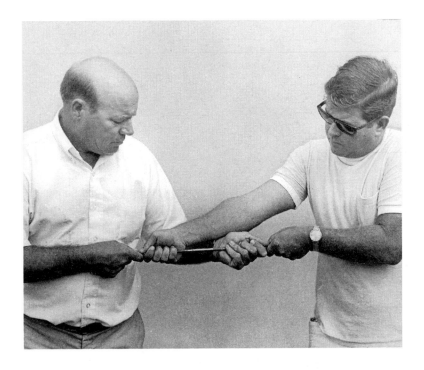

If you have a stuck rod and a companion to help, each person should place one hand on either side of the ferrule and then apply pressure. This insures that tension is applied in a straight line.

MARKING FLY LINES

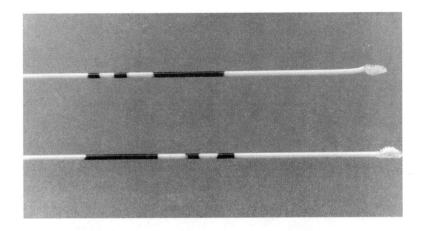

Fly lines look alike. Most fly fishermen own several — often more. Marking the line sizes is necessary. Using a permanent marking pen, you can identify the lines. A one-inch mark indicates the numeral five and a small ring indicates the numeral one. If you look at the two lines in the photo, you can see that each has one long mark and two small rings, meaning they are number seven lines. Note the nail knot at the right of the photo; this is the front of the line. The top line is a weight-forward seven line; the long mark is placed in the *forward* position. A double taper line, shown on the bottom, has the smaller mark in front and the larger mark behind it indicating a double-taper seven line which is *smaller* in the front.

If the line is very dark in color, you can take the line to an electrical supply store and buy shrink tubing that fits snugly over the line. Cut the required lengths, slide it on the line and while holding the shrink tubing in position, immerse it in boiling water for about 30 seconds. It will permanently set the tubing on the line, and the boiling water won't hurt the fly line.

39 TWO NECESSARY LINES FOR SALTWATER FLY FISHING

Two lines will help you meet almost all conditions in saltwater, whether it is fly fishing for stripers in New England or seeking tarpon in Costa Rica. Of course, there are many specialty lines that work wonderfully well under certain conditions. But, if you have a weight-forward floating line and a Teeny 300 fly line, you'll do well. The floater will work well for those times when you are throwing popping bugs or flies that swim within two or three feet of the surface. When you need to get the fly down lower, the Teeny 300 will do the job.

40 REMOVING COILS FROM FLY LINES

    Most fly lines, especially floating types, come off the reel in tight curls, making it difficult to cast. There is a very quick and easy method of removing these coils. Place the line under your foot, with about four feet on either side, as shown here, and then give a stout pull. Repeat the operation, in minutes you can remove the coils.

41 DAMAGING A FLY LINE

    The quickest way I know to ruin a fly line is to roll it underfoot as shown in this photo. Many times a fisherman will want to get the line from underfoot and slides the foot over the line to get it out of the way. This causes tight coils (as seen in the photo) that are permanent and make the line unusable.

42 WINDING IN FLY LINE

When winding in the fly line it will often spiral and tangle around the rod tip. This is because as we wind we wave the rod tip like a conductor's baton. If you place the tip underwater, as Charley Wells is doing here, or hold the tip against something soft, such as tall grass, the line will wind smoothly through the guides.

43 SHORT LEADERS ARE BEST WITH SINKING LINES

A long leader is a disadvantage when fishing with a sinking fly line. The extended leader causes the fly to swim well above the line, defeating the purpose the sinking line. Underwater, a long leader is not necessary. I rarely use a leader more than 4 feet in length when fishing with a sinking line. Here Bill Schoutta holds up a striped bass caught on a leader of 18 inches.

44 TRIM THOSE KNOTS

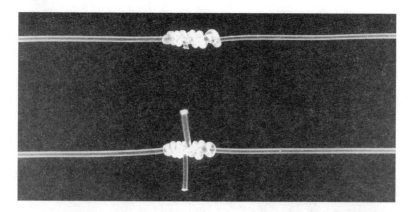

The knot at the top is properly trimmed. Too many people finish knots like the lower one with stubs sticking out that, when fighting a fish, can catch the leader on grass .

45 TESTING KNOTS

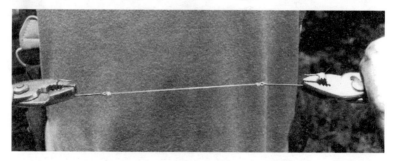

There is an easy, never fail method of making a comparison between the strength of two knots. Use two identical hooks and attach one knot to one hook and the other knot to the other hook. Then, use two pair of pliers. Grasp the hooks and jerk the line. Duplicate this test at least ten times to make sure of your observation. This will show you which knot is superior.

46 LEADER CLIPPER

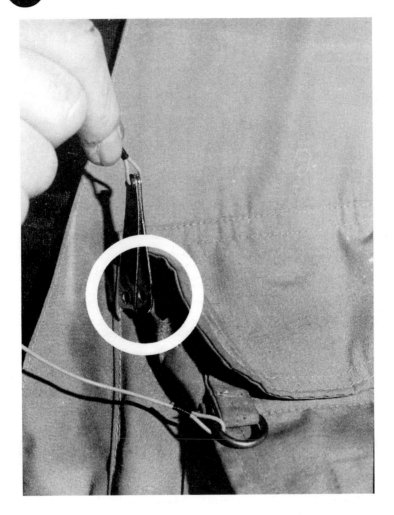

While you can buy a clipper to trim leader knots, a much less expensive model is a pair of inexpensive nail clippers, with the handle removed. Just hold the thumb and first finger over the cutting edge and apply pressure to cut the monofilament.

CHECKING FOR NICKS

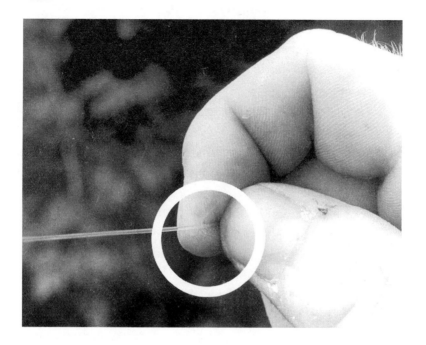

Monofilament has very low shear strength. A nick in monofilament vastly weakens the material. There is a simple way to check for nicks that may be hard to detect with the eye. Place the monofilament between the thumb and first finger. *Be sure to push* the thumbnail firmly against the mono, so it depresses into the first finger. Now draw the mono through your thumbnail and finger and you will detect even the slightest nick.

48 LEFTY'S LEADER FORMULA

The following chart represents a tapered leader formula that I urge you to try if you use a rod that casts a size 8 through 12 and you fish saltwater, Atlantic salmon, steelhead, bass or any fly fishing that requires longer casts and the ability to turn over a bulky or heavy fly.

The important factor is to recognize that the butt section is one-half the total length of the leader. Then short lengths are used to drop down to the tippet. If you feel that a 50-pound butt section is too heavy for you, start with 40 pound, and reduce the leader correspondingly.

Here is the reason for the butt section being one-half the length of the leader. As your line unrolls toward the target and arrives at the leader, you need enough flexible weight to make the leader continue to unroll. By using a heavy monofilament that is one half the length of the leader, you retain enough energy to turn over flies well.   (It is not recommended that you use this leader for trout fishing. Commercial leaders for trout, especially for dry flies, are suggested.)

Lefty's Tapered Leader Formula
50 pound butt = 50 % of leader

Length	50 lb.	40 lb.	30 lb.	20 lb.	15-12-10 lb.
10 ft.	5 ft.	1 ft.	1 ft.	1 ft.	2 ft.
12 ft.	6 ft.	2 ft.	1 ft.	1 ft.	2 ft.
14 ft.	7 ft.	3 ft.	1 ft.	1 ft.	2 ft.
16 ft.	8 ft.	4 ft.	1 ft.	1 ft.	2 ft.

49 BOGA GRIP

Bill Schoutta demonstrates the use of a Boga Grip. This is a commercial tool that gently lip holds any fish, so it can be safely lifted from the water, weighed, and the hook removed. It is available from many fishing shops and catalogs.

50 CARRY YOUR ROD BEHIND YOU

After you break your first rod walking through the woods, you learn never to carry it in front of you again. Always walk with the rod behind you. Be sure, too, to keep the leader and line tight against the rod to prevent it from snagging on brush.

51 PRESOAK SOME FLIES

Many streamer flies are difficult to get them to swim at the proper depth because they are made from buoyant materials, such as deer hair and wool. Realizing this, you can presoak the fly so that it will swim deep. Carry a small Zip Loc bag with you and before using the fly, place some water with the fly in the Zip Loc. When you want to fish it, it will be thoroughly soaked.

52 A GREAT INSECT SAMPLER

Trout fishermen have an advantage over the fish, if they know what the trout are feeding on. There are many gadgets that let you sample what is in the water. Most involve a net and a handle, which seems to always be tangled, torn or in some manner, unsatisfactory. Many years ago I started using an inexpensive soap dish (about 50 cents). Cut out the entire bottom, but leave about a one-quarter-inch ledge. Take a small piece of plastic window screening, you can often get scraps from the local hardware store and affix the screen to the ledge with either hot glue or epoxy.

The modified soapbox offers several advantages: it is easy to carry, doesn't cost much, takes up little room, is durable and once you catch insects in it, you can close the lid to trap them.

53 TAKE THE TEMPERATURE

Trout especially are affected by water temperature. They are not called cold water species without reason. During the summer months most streams heat up during the day and then cool off in the evening.

During the hottest part of summer, trout feed best in the morning when water temperatures are low. Gradually, during the day the sun heats the water and when temperatures get into

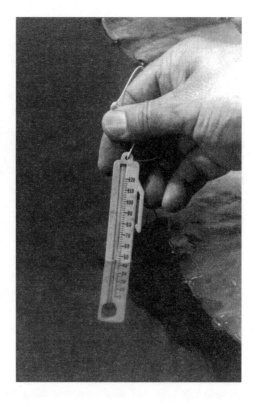

the 70-degree range, most trout slow down or stop feeding. A thermometer is an essential tool of the summer trout fisherman. You can usually get them from fly shops, but also, any good camera store will have easy to read and durable thermometers.

54 WADE SOFTLY

Water transmits sound about 4-½ times faster than air. This should tell you that when approaching fish (especially trout) you should stay out of the water to improve your chances of stalking the fish. Chuck Edghill illustrates how not to wade. Notice there are very visible waves moving away from his boots. If you must wade, wade slowly. A good check is to see that the surface waves around your boots are not radiating more than a foot. If they are, slow down.

55 A GUIDE CAN BE YOUR BEST FRIEND

Whenever you fish new waters, a guide is your best investment. The guide knows where the fish are, what flies to use, how to approach, and how to cast to the fish. Del Brown, right in the photo, is one of the best all around fly fishermen I know. He fishes New Zealand's rivers every year. Yet, he realizes that a guide will help him catch more fish and have more fun.

56 DRAG-FREE DRIFT

Getting a drag-free drift with your fly is essential to catching trout. In fast water like this, John Zajano demonstrates that dropping your fly line over a rock, helps insure a long, drag-free drift.

DON'T GIVE YOURSELF AWAY

Fish see things very well projecting above the surface close to them. This angler is doing it right. He is staying out of the water and is keeping his profile low as he casts for trout.

58 USE THE SHADE

This angler reduced his chances of catching trout. By standing in the sunlight as he casts, the trout has a good chance of seeing him.

The same angler casting from the shade is less likely to be seen by the trout.

59 PERFECTING YOUR ACCURACY

To catch many fish we need to be accurate. One of the best ways I know to improve your accuracy, is to use a mousetrap. Lay the trap cocked to go off, about 25 feet away. Attach a weighted fly with the bend of the hook removed to your fly rod. You need a weighted fly to set off the trap. Even the top fly fishermen won't hit the trap often, so don't expect to. But what will happen is this: as you make more casts you will gradually find that *all* your casts are much closer. Not only will you improve your accuracy, but also, you will have fun doing it.

60 IMPROVING YOUR LOOP CONTROL

A hula hoop is a great tool to help you tighten your casting loop. Attach the hula hoop to a pole (as shown) or have a friend hold it. Stand about 25 feet from the hula hoop. Make sure no fly is attached to the leader. Usually, the first several casts will not go through the hoop. But since you are mentally monitoring each cast, you will soon discover that your loops start to tighten and you begin throwing through the hoop with some regularity. When you can throw about 70 per cent of your casts through, move back a little and try again. Soon, you'll be able to put some loops through even as far away as 40 or 50 feet!

DON'T USE THE ROD TIP TO MANIPULATE YOUR FLY

King Montgomery demonstrates the right and wrong way to retrieve the fly. In the above photo he flips the rod tip to manipulate a streamer fly or popping bug. The arrow points to the slack that accumulates when this is done.

In the photo below, King shows you the proper method of retrieving with a fly rod, by keeping the rod low and pointed at the water. Use the line hand to manipulate the fly. Note the rod tip is almost in the water and a straight line results. This insures a better chance to hook the fish on a strike.

62 MAKING A BETTER RETRIEVE

Photo 62A

Bob Clouser demonstrates a basic mistake in retrieving an underwater fly and how to correct it. In Photo 62A he has made a cast, and as his fly swims downstream, Bob *keeps the rod pointed where the cast ended*. The rod remains stationary, while the current pushes a big bag in his fly line. This results in two undesirable factors. One, there is considerable slack if he tries to set the hook. Two, the bag creates extra tension on the fly, so that it swims unnaturally fast.

In Photo 62B Bob ended the cast as in the first photo in this sequence. But as the line drifts downstream, Bob moves the rod downstream. He is trying to maintain a straight line with no bag in it.

Photo 62B

In Photo 62C Bob continues to make the rod follow the line. Note that the line remains straight throughout the drift. If a fish should strike, there is so little slack in the line that a good hook up results.

Shown in Photo 62D is another method to get a draft free drift by rolling the rod tip upstream. This forms an upstream mend and a good drift is possible.

CASTING IN TIGHT QUARTERS

Many times, when trout fishing on small streams, you find a hot spot you would like to cast into where there isn't enough room to work a longer rod. Larry Kreh demonstrates a simple trick to reduce your rod length by more than a foot. Slide the hand up to the stripping or butt guide. Make the cast. When the cast ends, move the hand back to the rod handle and continue to fish. This trick has allowed me to fish many places I couldn't otherwise.

GETTING A STUCK FLY OFF A LOG

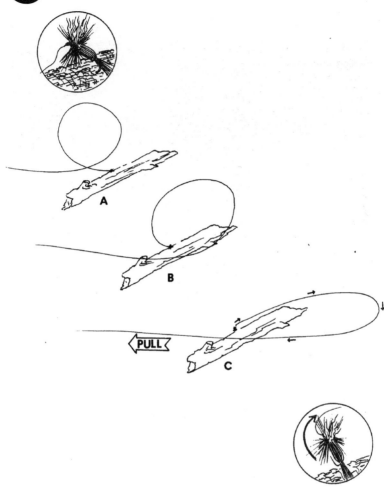

Frequently, we will over cast and snag the fly on a log or other debris. Not always, but most of the time you can free it easily. Make a roll cast well above the snagged fly. When the line rolls behind the log and the leader and line are still in the air, make a hard backcast. This usually pulls on the fly from the opposite direction, and the fly comes free.

EXTENDING YOUR CASTING DISTANCE

Bob Clouser demonstrates how to throw the full length of a fly line.

Here is something just about every fly caster is familiar with. He wants to reach a target a little father than he normally casts. Two false casts are made and they look pretty good — nice loops and a tight line. Then, the final cast is made and everything goes to pieces.   Why?

The only thing that will make your line go farther is how short and fast you accelerate the tip at the final moment of the cast, and how quickly you stop it. The reason why most casters fail on extended casts is that extra power and distance is put into the final moment of the cast. This destroys the loop and throws energy around a circle.

Here is how you can increase your own distance. Make two false casts with as much line as you can handle and still get good loop control. *Do not put one more ounce of effort into the cast with the rod hand, but make your double haul faster.* The haul does only one thing. It makes the tip move faster.

Here is what you will accomplish. Because you did not put extra force in the rod hand, the loop will remain tight, as it did when false casting. By accelerating the tip with a faster haul on the line, you increase line speed and you will find you will be able to throw farther and easier.

66 TO HOLD A FISH

The above photo shows one way to hold a fish when removing the hook. Instead of squeezing the fish and harming it, simply turn it upside down as shown here. Most of the time the fish will simply lie there.

67 THE COMFORT LIFT

Another method of handling fish was shown to me in Australia. It is called the comfort lift. Slide your hand under the fish and locate the *center of the fish's body weight* — not the center of the fish. Be sure to grasp the fish from the belly side, so the dorsal spines don't prick you. Slowly lift the fish from the water, as Ted Juracsik is doing. If the fish starts to slide to your left, simply lower the fish and move the hand a little to the left until you establish the center of the fish's weight. Using the comfort lift you can gently hold a fish out of the water and totally immobile.

68 THE VERTICAL HOLD

There are some species that have no sharp teeth that are immobilized by holding them by the lip, such as the snook (shown here), bass and barramundi. However, the fish should be held vertically like this. If you grip a fish like this and tilt the head up, it is possible to break the jaw of the fish.

TO HOLD SHORT FISH

Any short fish, such as panfish and snappers, have very sharp spines. When you handle one of these species, it is best to slide the hand toward the fish from the belly and grip the fish as shown.

70 TO HOLD SALTWATER SPECIES

Any of the jack species in saltwater can be paralyzed without harm to the fish by gripping it across the head, as shown here. Press the first finger and thumb against the fish's body where the gill covers come together at the top of the body.

71 POINTING THE ROD

When you stand on the bow of a flats boat your guide will tell you where to look at a fish that he has spotted. The quickest way for you to locate the fish is to point your rod towards it. Then have the guide tell you to move your rod to the right or left, until he says stop. You will be aiming the rod at the fish.

72 WADING PROPERLY

In Photo 72A, Jeannie Carley demonstrates the proper way to wade a saltwater flat. As she moves forward, she slides her foot along, in contact with the bottom.

In Photo 72B, she demonstrates the wrong way to wade a flat. By raising her foot in a normal walking manner and placing it forward, she could step on a stingray hidden in the bottom.

Photo 72A

This could mean a hospital trip. But, sliding the foot along the bottom, *if the foot contacts the bottom*, the ray flees and the angler is unharmed.

Photo 72B

73 TEASE THOSE FISH TO THE FLY

If you fly fish the tropics, you should consider carrying a spinning rod with a chugger-type fishing lure that has the hooks removed. The chugger, when cast out and retrieved with sharp jerks on the rod, splashes a lot of water and makes loud sounds.

One angler works the chugger attracting the fish to the lure. The fly caster throws his fly or popping bug beside the chugger and gets immediate strikes on many tropical species.

74 BE READY FOR BREAKING FISH

When you race up to fish breaking on the surface in saltwater, you can gain considerable advantage if you do what Bob Clouser is showing here. Get in the corner of the boat and allow about 20 to 30 feet of fly line and leader to dangle behind the racing boat. When the boat stops, sweep the rod forward and make an immediate cast.

75 TAKE ALONG A FLY SWATTER

Biting flies can ruin a pleasant day in saltwater flats. I now take a fly swatter to kill them. It can change a bad day into a good one.

76 MY FAVORITYE WADING BASKET

A wading basket is necessary for many saltwater fishing situations. The post popular is a dishpan type that is suspended in front of the fly fisherman. My personal favorite is a cut down office wastebasket. It is suspended from the shoulder with a strap and attached to the leg. This allows the angler to move, even run down the beach, with the line securely inside. Also, the number of holes in the basket let water immediately flow out.

77 THE LINE TAMER

The Line Tamer is a commercial product that is ideal for anglers who fish the flats. The unit, available from many fly shops, allows you to store line during a retrieve and almost always flows freely out on the forward cast. When you change locations, simply deposit the rod in it with the line inside and run to the next location. Pick up the rod and you are ready to cast.

78 GETTING MORE LINE FAST

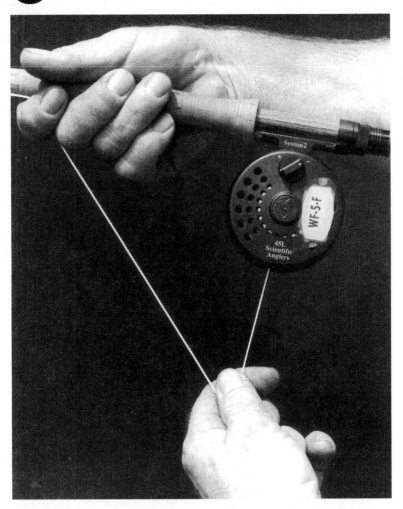

If you are retrieving a streamer fly or popping bug and you need more line for the next cast, you can strip off additional line as you retrieve the fly. *Grasp both the line coming from the reel and what is being retrieved and strip both at the same time.* On the next cast, the extra line you had pulled from the spool while retrieving is available.

79 WHEN A FISH RUNS UNDER THE BOAT

casa mar

If you are in a boat and the fish you are fighting darts under the boat to the other side, don't try to remain where you are. It could mean a broken rod. Here, Cathy Beck shows how to push the rod tip into the water and sweep around to the other side, to continue fighting the fish.

HOW TO FISH A FARM POND RIGHT AND WRONG

Photo 80A

Mark Lamos shows in Photo 80A how not to fish a farm pond. By backcasting over the bank, the line may tangle in the bushes — or in this case, the tree behind him.

Photo 80B shows that by backcasting over the water, you're less like to snag the backcast behind you.

Photo 80B

81 LEARN WHERE TO FISH FOR TROUT

When trout fishing, if you are not sure where to fish the most productive water, look for flowing lines of foam. Most of the insects that wash into the pool from upstream will be in these foam lines. They represent the major current flows coming through the pool.

82 A COMMON MISTAKE THAT RUINS YOUR PRESENTATION

The angler demonstrates a major reason why fly fishermen don't catch fish. Surface tension grips the fly line on the water. When you make the backcast, be sure *all line* is off the water before making the backcast. If any of it remains, it will be ripped from the surface and the resultant noise can spook any fish.

83 CRUSHING THE BARB CORRECTLY

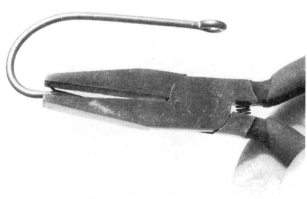

Many fly fishermen now crush the barb on the hook to make for an easy release of the fish. But, many highly tempered hooks often break when the barb is depressed. To prevent this from happening, grasp the pliers or hemostats so that the tip of the pliers clasp the hook both in front and behind the barb. This way the metal is well supported and you'll eliminate breaking the hook.

84 CHECKING HOOK FOR SHARPNESS

A sharp hook is essential to effective fly fishing. If you are in doubt about the point, drag it with light pressure across the thumbnail. If it doesn't dig in, it is time to resharpen it.

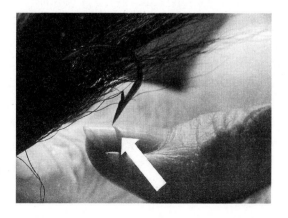

85 THREE HOOK SHARPENING TOOLS

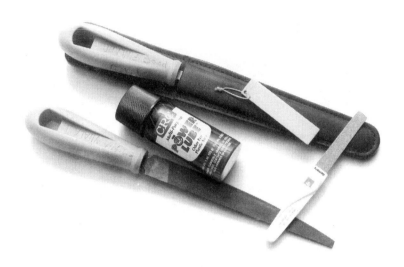

Pictured here are three good hook sharpening tools. At the top is a Nicholson 6-inch smooth file, stored in a leather case. By saturating the file with CRC or WD-40 and storing it in the case, the file can be used around saltwater often for several years before it will rust.

Lying on the leather case is a white, ceramic stone sold by Tiemco. I don't use this for original sharpening. Because it will never rust, I carry it when wading in saltwater, or on the boat, to touch up a dulled point.

The small tool at the right of the photo is a diamond dust (usually silicone carbide) fingernail file available in most drug stores. One side has very fine grit and the other side slightly more coarse. The finer side will sharpen flies as small as size 24. The more coarse side will work for hooks to about size 2.

86 PUNCHING GLUE AND PAINT OUT OF HOLES

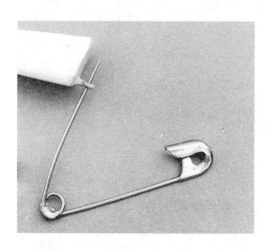

Hook eyes clogged with glue or paint should not be opened with the point of a hook, which may dull it. Instead, carry a few safety pins for the job. One pinned to a trout fly fishing vest is always handy.

87 HOW TO DETERMINE THE WEIGHT OF YOUR SINKING FLY

Many streamers and nymphs are often weighted differently. To signify whether the fly is unweighted, lightly or heavily weighted, try this. You can use thread to properly mark each fly, like we have done in the photo. The top fly is unweighted and has no band of thread. The middle fly is lightly weighted with a narrow ring of light thread. The bottom fly is heavily weighted with a ring of darker thread.

SEEING DRY FLIES BETTER

Most fishermen are now casting smaller dry flies, which can often be tough to see on the surface. If you are using a parachute or thorax tied dry fly, try this. Take one or two strands of pearl Krystal Flash (which is spiraled Mylar). Fold the Krystal Flash a number of times, and then construct the wing from it. Clip the ends after the fly is completed to form a wing as shown here. Note that the material spirals. Because it is highly reflective and twisted, it will be easy for the angler to see even at a distance.

89 USING BRAIDED WIRE TIPPETS

A short length of braided wire in front of the fly prevents cut offs from sharp teeth. The figure 8 knot is generally used to attach the wire to the hook. However, when closing the knot, you should pull all slack from the tag end of the wire. If you pull on the main wire, it distorts as the knot is tightened. The crimped wire is drawn in front of the fly, as shown in the photo of the middle fly. This will cause the fly to swim unnaturally on the retrieve. The bottom photo shows how straight the wire remains if applying pressure only to the tag end to tighten the knot.

A GREAT STREAMER FLY STORAGE BAG

My favorite way of storing my streamer flies is with a gadget designed to carry a bass fisherman's plastic worms. When carrying larger flies, the individual panels should be at least seven inches long. This permits you to store long flies easily. The bags are inexpensive and will enable you to carry more than 100 flies. The advantages to this storage bag is that when opened, all flies are visible, and easy to get to. If you travel, when folded, it is compact and easily stored in your luggage or on a boat. They can be purchased from bass fishing shops.

91 SAFE KEEPING YOUR FLY

When
carrying any
streamer flies or
popping bugs (I
don't recommend
this for dry flies),
you can safely
store the hook
under the reel
seat hood, as
shown here. This
protects the fly,

but also prevents the fisherman from stabbing the hand when the
fly is placed in the conventional ring keeper.

92 KEEP SAMPLES

Keep a sample
fly whenever you
find a special one
that is effective in
certain waters. That
way you can always
get more. Even if
you don't tie, one of
your friends or a
local fly shop owner

can find someone to duplicate your sample. Take notes on
individual flies if you feel they are necessary. I have been doing
this for years and it has paid off for me.

93 CARRY ONLY WHAT YOU NEED

A box full of flies with rusty hooks is the result of carrying all of them with you when wading. If you fall down, that's sure to result in many flies being soaked and ruined. Instead, hang a small block of closed cell foam around your neck. Stick in the foam block only the flies you will need while wading . They are easy to get to, and you won't ruin a box of flies if you fall in.

94 NEVER PUT TACKLE ON THE ROOF

The angler placing his outfit on the top of the car will one day lose it. If you want to be sure you don't drive off and leave tackle, always place it on the hood, so it can be easily seen.

KEEP YOUR NAPKINS DRY

I am constantly cleaning my polarizing glasses. Rain, sweat and salt spray while riding in a boat, all saturate your napkins. I carry several in a Zip Loc bag where they remain clean and dry.

ALWAYS ANCHOR A CANOE FROM THE BACK

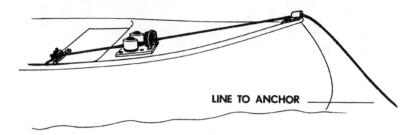

LINE TO ANCHOR

If I were limited to one watercraft for my freshwater fishing, it would be a canoe. Easily transportable and with it, you can go almost anywhere. But, if you anchor a canoe in fast water, never tie the anchor line to the side of the craft — it will surely turn over.

The drawing indicates the safest way to use an anchor in a canoe. The end of the anchor rope is attached beside the seat. Use a rope clamp (available at a sailing supply store). Run the rope through it and secure it. The eyelet at the back can also be purchased at a sailing supply store. The anchor hangs outside (no dirt or water gets in the boat when the anchor is not in use). By releasing the rope lock you can lower or raise the anchor at will.

97 END THOSE CLEAT PROBLEMS

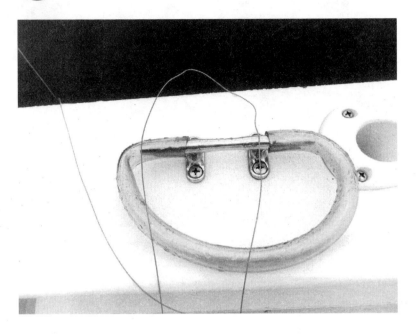

Cleats on boats will constantly grab your fly line, often at the worst time. To prevent that from happening, purchase a short length of the proper diameter hose and attach to each end of the cleat. Force the tubing to lie flush with the boat surface and your problems are over. If you want to secure a rope to the cleat, there is no need to remove the tubing, simply raise the curved portion, attach the rope and let the tubing fall back into place.

98 ELIMINATE STRAP NOISE AND A CAR TOP CARRIER TRICK

Many people transporting car top boats are using the popular foam blocks, shown here. From experience I learned that you should tighten the back of the boat down first — then the front. If you tighten the front strap first and then pull down on the back ones, you may not get the back ones as tight as possible. If this happens, one or both of the back support foam blocks may be slip out when under way.

Straps can make a bothersome noise, especially when they are drawn very tight. The wind works on a taut strap much as your fingers strumming a guitar string. To eliminate this annoying noise, put one or two twists in the strap, as you can see on the top of the canoe in the photo.

99 USE NETTING TO SAVE CASTS

Many boats have line-entangling devices. A piece of netting thrown over them will allow you to cast worry free. I favor netting about six to seven feet square. It should have some small sinkers around the edge to hold it in place. If you can't find a commercial fishing supply store that has the netting, you can use a minnow seine, available in many fishing tackle stores.

100 CHECK THOSE TRAILER TIRES

I used to think that trailer tires were the worst of all tires —
they kept failing me. It was my fault. Most trailer tires are
tubeless. Under long periods of storage the tires tend to flatten
slightly at the bottom from the boat's weight. This causes a small
amount of air to leak from the tire. You can eliminate most
trailer tire problems by purchasing inexpensive inner tubes for
your tires. When you trail a boat with tires that are not up to
recommended pressure, they tend to flex badly. This constant
flexing build up excessive heat that will destroy your tire. You
need to keep the correct pressure in the tires, so they remain in
their normal shape when pulling your boat.

You need to check your tires with a gauge before you move the trailer. If the trailer has set for any period of time, the tires will surely be a little lower than normal. *Note how much lower the pressure is in each tire.* As an example, suppose that both tires were four pounds low. Because they are under inflated, when you get to the first air pump, and you take another reading it will be higher. Remember that each tire was four pounds low before you moved. Add four pounds to each tire.

If you do this, you'll be amazed at how long your tires will last.

 ## TO EASILY BACK A TRAILER

Many people have difficulty when backing a trailer. Much of this is because if you want the trailer to go to the left, you must move the steering wheel to the right. However, if you position your hand on the *bottom* of the steering wheel instead of the top, you can then move the steering the same direction you want the boat to go.